Keeping It Real:
The Different Mask
We Wear in Church

Keeping It Real: The Different Mask We Wear in Church

Pastor Tereasa Brown

To order additional copies of this book, contact:
Xlibris
1-888-795-4274
www.Xlibris.com
Orders@Xlibris.com
780474

CONTENTS

This book is dedicated to my children Alexus, Diamond, Calvin, Tatyana; and my grandsons Jeremiah and Morrell Jr. You children motivate me to be the best I can be. You're the reason I work so hard. I love you all. God did it again!

Acknowledgments

First, I want to thank God for trusting me to be his mouthpiece and for reigning favor over my children and me. Also, I want to thank my mother Geraldine for always having a listening ear; for praying for me through storms and valleys; and for pushing me to be the best pastor, preacher, and teacher of the word of God. My mother always tells me "before I sell out, get out!" I also want to thank my church family Spread the Word Ministries of Kansas for their encouragement. Last, I want to thank my spiritual family, who continues to lift me in prayer.

Introduction

We are living in the last days, and people's souls are at stake. As pastors, preachers, and teachers of the gospel, we are obligated to preach the unadulterated word of God. In this book, I only speak about the numerous churches I've visited or have been a member of. All churches do not operate like this, but there are many churches here in America that deal with some of these very issues that I highlight in this book.

God is going to hold the leadership in the church accountable for how we've allowed business to be conducted in the church. As 1Peter 4:17 says, "For the time is come that judgement must begin at the house of God: and if it first begin at us, what shall the end be of them that obey not the gospel of God?" Prayerfully, those who read this book don't get mad at me for touching on certain subjects but get mad enough at themselves to change the way they operate as children of God. When we know better, we are to do better. Be blessed and enjoy.

PART I

When the Church Celebrates Halloween

TRICK OR TREAT

We who are saints of God or who claim Christianity tend to call Halloween a pagan holiday. We say it glorifies the devil and all matter of evilness. The world celebrates this one day by having Halloween parties, putting on costumes and masks, dressing up like one's favorite movie or television show characters, going to haunted houses, and probably the most common, going trick-or-treating.

Now we know how the world celebrates Halloween for one day out of the year. Now let's look at how the church celebrates Halloween all year long. "Be wary of false preachers who smile a lot, dripping with practiced sincerity. Chances are they are out to rip you off some way or other. Don't be impressed with charisma; look for character. Who preachers are is the main thing, not what they say. A genuine leader will never exploit your emotions or your pocketbook. These diseased trees with their bad apples are going to be chopped and burned" (Matthew 7:15-20 MSG).

It's sad that we have these types of preachers, prophets, and leaders in our churches. They run in circles. They invite one another to their respective churches to pick the pockets of their flock. They start off preaching the word of God, and somewhere in the message, they take the word of God out of context. Any time you take the word of God out of context and drop the text, you're left with nothing but a con (that's the trick). Then the prophesies start flowing, and the preacher of the hour is prophesying to people that God's going to give them a house, car, money, and land. Never does the prophesy come to the people about their character or their conduct (that's the treat), and everyone is jumping and shouting. The preacher will prophesy to you about worldly wealth, but all the while, you're spiritually impoverished. "For what shall it profit a man, if he shall gain the whole world, and lose his own soul?" (Mark 8:36 KJV).

As charismatic as the preacher is and as good as the preacher preaches and prophesies, you have to make sure that what they are saying lines up with the word of God. You must read the word of God for yourself and have a prayer life so that when foolishness from the pulpit comes to you, you'll know it's not for you. No doubt many of these preachers are counting on you being caught up in the moment so that you don't really realize that they are picking your pockets. They are counting on the emotionalism of the moment, the tears streaming down the faces of the people, the hopelessness of the people, and, of course, the keyboardist and organist hitting just the right keys that church people love to hear. Now that the atmosphere is set for trick-or-treating, let the games and gimmicks begin. All we need now are some popcorn, candy, and soda because it's going to be quite the show.

I'm Counting on You Not to Read the Word

The Lord said sow a seed of $500, and by the time you get home, your blessing is going to meet you there. Line up right here to sow your $500 seed. This is just in, hot off the press from heaven, even if you don't have the $500 seed. Get with a neighbor on your row, put your money together, and come up with the $500 seed, and God is going to give you a double blessing. I know no one wants to miss out on this blessing, and if you don't have the $500 seed and you and your neighbor on your row can't come up with it but you may have a $350 seed, you can line up right here.

Someone may be saying they only have a $100 seed or a $50 seed. God will bless you with that as well. Then there are those in the congregation who don't have anything to give, and they sit there, feeling like God will not bless them because they have no money. These preachers disguise this auction they are having in the church as a God-ordained offering. This type of foolishness happens all year long.

Some pastors, preachers, prophets, and leaders prey on the vulnerable church members who want something so bad from God that they believe anything that comes across the pulpit. These same people who give their money, believing the auction that was held in the church, have a hard time getting money from the church when they fall on hard times. In fact, they have to go through the deacon board and the trustee board. They have to explain why they've fallen on hard times. The deacons and trustees look at the books to see if the person is a tithe-paying member, and the leadership as a whole have the nerve to say things such as "We are not a social services or welfare agency." Mind you, these people didn't have to go through anyone to give their money to the pastor who tricked them into giving. And we wonder why finances are a sore subject when we relate it to the church.

"Each of you should give what you have decided in your heart to give, not reluctantly or under compulsion, for God loves a cheerful giver" (2Corinthians 9:7 NIV). So if the Bible says we have already purposed in our hearts what we are going to give to the church and not for us to give grudgingly or out of compulsion, why does the very person holding the auction in the church never read this scripture in its entirety? Why do they just skip to the end that says, "God loves a cheerful giver?" Now they will read 2Corinthians 9:6: "Remember this: whosoever sows sparingly will also reap sparingly, and whosoever sows generously will also reap generously" (NIV). This is how they play on the emotions of the people and their pocketbook. They tell you part of the word. Telling you part of the word is like telling you half of the truth, and a half truth is a whole lie. I cannot stress it enough; you have to read and study the word of God for yourself. You don't need a title in the church to read, understand, and get a revelation of the word from God.

Have you ever wondered what the church is doing with the tithes and the offerings they collect without the gimmicks and auctions—besides paying the pastor, the church mortgage, utilities, and church staff—if they are on the payroll? Some people feel as though the pastor should not get paid, and that's not biblical. Actually, the Bible says in 1 Timothy 5:17-18, "The elders who direct the affairs of the church well are worthy of double honor, especially those whose work is preaching and teaching. For scripture says, do not muzzle an ox while it is treading out the grain, and the worker deserves his wage" (NIV).

Is the church giving back to the community that helped them build the church because of their generous giving? Is the church being a good steward over the tithes and offerings? If they are, then why are there auctions held in the church? And why are the puppets allowed in the pulpit, and who's pulling the strings? When did money become more important than souls? Souls are doomed to hell, and no one is ministering to their souls. They are only ministering to their emotions. People are leaving the church because it's become all about the money.

The saints are sitting in the house of God Sunday after Sunday, thinking it's okay to sin because no one is preaching on their sin. No one is saying, "Repent for the kingdom of God is at hand" (Matthew 3:2 KJV). They are just preaching, "Give and you'll be blessed."

You have to wonder when do the pastors change their robes for their Halloween costumes. Is it when they see how other pastors are reaping the benefits by holding auctions? Perhaps they are watching televangelists and want what they see. Maybe it can be they feel the church is not paying them enough, so they resort to gimmicks and tricks to get what they feel they deserve. Whatever the reason is, God is not pleased.

> God's message came to me: Son of man prophesy against the shepherd-leaders of Israel. Yes, prophesy! Tell those shepherds, God, the Master, says: Doom to you shepherds of Israel, feeding your own mouths! Aren't shepherds supposed to feed sheep? You drink the milk, you make clothes from the wool, you roast the lambs, but you don't feed the sheep. You don't build up the weak ones, don't heal the sick, don't doctor the injured, don't go after the strays, don't look for the lost. You bully and badger them. And now they're scattered every which way because there was no shepherd-scattered and easy pickings for wolves and coyotes. Scattered-my sheep!-exposed and vulnerable across mountains and hills. My sheep all over the world, and no one out looking for them. (Ezekiel 34: 1-6 MSG)

Instead of doing things the world's way when it comes to the people of God, how about we do things the way the Bible instructs us to do them? "Defend the poor and fatherless: do justice to the afflicted and needy." (Psalms 82:3) Nowhere in the Bible does it tell us to swindle the people out of their money or prophesy to them things God didn't say. When all we want is the people's money, we are bringing a disgrace on the church and the name of God.

We are acting like crooked businessmen and businesswomen in the church. We are causing "church hurt," and there's no hurt such as church hurt. I sometimes wonder, *Have the leaders in the church actually counted the souls they've destroyed and have become stumbling blocks to them because of money and false prophesies?*

It Must Be You

When you've been lied to about a prophecy and you talk to the person who tricked you out of your money, they will tell you, "Maybe it's you, maybe you don't have enough faith to receive the prophecy, and maybe your life is not lining up with the word of God." Never do you hear them say, "Maybe I got it wrong and didn't hear from

God." They place the unfulfilled prophesy on you and never offer you a refund. Your money has been collected and spent, and they are cooking up another gimmick to get more money out of you.

THE HAUNTED HOUSE

Church used to be a place where we come to get a word
and pray,
Now it's a place where we put our mask on and play.
We play with people's emotions to get money,
We play with people's souls, and that's not even funny.
We're quick to denounce gays and call them all sorts of
names,
While we look past church corruption and rise to fame.
We don't speak on the pastor who beats his wife,
The deacon who's a drunk,
The leader who sleeps around with church members,
And the church mother that curses.
Oh, what a shame!
We wonder why sinners look at us crazy when we say,
"Bless His name."
We need to practice what we preach and turn from our
wicked ways.
You never know, our soul could be called on the carpet
today.
REPENT! So that the Lord can hear our cries;
Because if we don't, one thing is for sure, in hell will we
lift up our eyes.

PART II

The Mask the First Lady Wears

To all pastors' wives who stand by their husbands through thick and thin, ups and downs, highs and lows, and ins and outs; to the first ladies who stand tall and know how to weather the storm of church folks and their foolishness, be blessed and stay encouraged.

And let us not be weary in well doing: for in due season we shall reap, if we faint not.

—Galatians 6:9—

The Blatant
Love Affair

Every first lady knows that the church is her husband's "real wife." The first lady is just the chick on the side. She's the lady whom the pastor comes to see once he has wrapped up his business with everyone else for the day.

She prepares him dinner but finds herself dining alone. She waits for him to come home but finds herself blowing out the candles and going to bed alone, only to be awaken in the middle of the night to meet the pastor's needs before he goes back to his "real wife." In no way, shape, form, or fashion is she smiling. No doubt she has some choice words for him, and since they are in the comfort of their own home, with no other eyes watching them, they are having a very unholy discussion.

When you talk to many first ladies, they will tell you that they didn't sign up to be the side chick. They will tell you that watching their husbands be present for the people and absent for the family isn't a walk in the park. The first lady has to watch this love affair up close. Everyone needs her man, and he tries his best to give them what they need. However, the one woman who really needs him has to stand on the sideline, wait for the crowd to leave all the while cheering him on, smiling on the outside and dying on the inside.

Because her husband does not hide this love affair and often openly speaks about it, it makes one wonder, "What is the real issue?" The irony of this is the first lady encourages her husband to love the other woman. She prays for him after the other woman disappoints him. She lifts his spirit, picks up the broken pieces, and helps him look good so he can shine in the face of the other woman.

It's not that often that the pastor says thank you to the first lady for understanding that he just can't walk out on his real wife. It's not that often the pastor thanks the first lady for understanding that his real wife will come first the majority of the times, and it may feel like she's being flaunted in her face. It's also not that often when he thanks her for embracing his real wife and for continuing to stand by his side day after day, Sunday after Sunday.

Speaking of Sunday, that's about the only day of the week that the first lady gets her props and is acknowledged in public. The pastor mentions her before he preaches as a gesture to tell his real wife that "If you don't act right, the first lady will, and I will make you the chick on the side instead of the first lady." If the first lady happens not to be in church when the pastor acknowledges her, just know she refuses to put the mask on today. She refuses to dress up in character. She's had it up to here with the church and the pastor. She will put her mask back on but not today.

The first lady sits and attentively listens while her husband preaches. His real wife is yelling, "Preach, Pastor!" and "Amen!" The first lady sits there and thinks, *If they only knew what I knew, they'd run for the hills. Many people in the church only see the man in the pulpit, but they have no idea about the man at home.*

Some pastors are physically, emotionally, financially, and psychologically abusive to their wives. They molest their children, drink heavily, and sleep around with women in the church. As Sunday service comes to a close, the pastor kisses his real wife goodbye and heads home with his chick on the side. He expects her to treat him like a king while he inadvertently allowed his real wife to treat her like a peasant.

Graciously, the first lady attends to all the pastor needs and manages to keep a smile on her face. She has inner strength like none other. On the outside, she may appear weak, but she is not a lady to be messed with. The first lady is a wise woman. She's not your ordinary, uncouth chick on the side. She never brings dishonor to her husband, his pastorship, the church, or herself. In fact, she treats her husband's real wife with the utmost dignity and respect. Because she knows her husband loves his real wife, she embraces the other woman.

Resenting being the chick on the side, the first lady learns how to keep her feelings and emotions in check. She never lets the other woman see how she truly feels. She has perfected the poker face. No one can read her. Silently, she takes her cares, hurts, disappointments, fears, and troubles to the Lord. Behind closed doors, she voices her concerns to her husband who may or may not take her feelings and concerns into consideration. One thing's for sure—the first lady can never let the other woman see that she's gotten to her because the other woman won't let up and will do her best to destroy her and exploit all her weaknesses.

You may ask, "What makes the first lady keep pushing and enduring such trauma by the actions of her husband?" Love, character, and reverential fear. She loves her husband with his flaws and all. Her word is her bond, so her character won't allow her to tuck tail and run at the sign of trouble. Ultimately, she fears the Lord. She made a vow between God, her husband, and the church. She took stock of the situation and counted up the cost and determined that although it would be very expensive, she would work diligently to meet the payments, no matter how much it would cost her.

She resolved within herself that she was making an investment, and that investment does not turn a profit overnight. She came into the marriage, understanding that her stock was high but some days she would feel that it had lost some value and ask the Lord, "Why me?" She came in, understanding that even when she would feel her stock was low, she could always bounce back; it would only be a matter of time. So this blatant love affair that her husband is having doesn't move her the same way that it moves another woman. She understands that being submissive to her husband is in no way a sign of weakness but a sign of strength and obedience to God.

For those of you who look at the first lady as weak, you are sadly mistaken. The church might be her husband's real wife, but he trusts his heart and feels safe with her.

Her husband and her children rise up and call her blessed. Her husband knows she brings him favor. He is well aware that many men in the church are just waiting for him to slip up, make a mistake, and leave her for the other woman so that they can partake in the goodness and kindness that the first lady bestows upon him; therefore, sometimes he does not mind stepping out on his real wife to be with his chick on the side. She can do for him what the real wife can't. She can make him feel good about himself when the real wife leaves him feeling empty.

Many women in the church calls the first lady names, speaking all manner of evil against her and starting all sorts of rumors about her, all the while secretly wishing they were in her shoes. They wish the pastor would glance at them or make them the chick on the side. They wish they could trade places with her and be the center of attraction and attention.

The problem is they will have to work really hard to be the woman that the first lady is. Because of the anointing of God on her life, she does it with grace. The first lady lives

1Corinthians 13:4-7 (NLT): "Love is patient and kind. Love is not jealous or boastful or proud or rude. It does not demand its own way. It is not irritable, and it keeps no record of being wronged. It does not rejoice about injustice but rejoices whenever truth wins out. Love never gives up, never loses faith, is always hopeful, and endures through every circumstance." The first lady truly loves her husband and his real wife. However, with all her love she pours out, she's still treated like the invisible woman.

The First Lady's Talk with God

I thought I could change him,

So I took his last name;

But with the people chanting and cheering,

All he saw was the glory and fame.

The more I loved him,

The more he clung to her.

He talked about her openly and paraded her in my face.

LORD! I'm the first lady, I don't want to catch a case.

He loves her unconditionally and says he's doing a work for you,

But I thought by taking his last name, I'd be his boo.

Lord, help me to see your vision, your purpose, and your plan

Before I wake up tomorrow and walk away from my destiny
and this man.

I understand, you calling him to be a preacher, but now he's
pastoring a church.

Lord, couldn't you have pulled me to the side to discuss this
first?

I know your thoughts are not my thoughts

Nor your ways are my ways,

So I'll stop complaining and be the good first lady and obey.

You Want Something from Me

You want me to smile and grin as if everything were fine,
When I'm sitting here wondering if I'm yours and you're
mine.
One false step and now there's a scandal, and everyone
knows the news.
Yet it's me—your rib, your rock— still sitting on the
front pew.
Many women in the church look as to say, "How could
you stand for him to be in your face?"
I'm wise enough to know they are the ones that want to
take my place.
I go to God with a tear-stained face and say, "Lord, how
can you let this be?"
And his reply is "My grace is sufficient for thee."
God asks, "Do you care what people say or what I see?

Well, let's talk about how YOU cheated on me.

You put shopping, girls' night out, your career, and kids before me;

And when I called your name, you were too tired, so I let you be.

You never saw your wrong.

You only saw his faults.

You never said a word,

But I knew your very thoughts.

I keep calling you to come closer to me, yet you keep pushing me further away.

I understand you want your freedom,

So I won't make you stay.

Go ahead. Go. Be free.

I'll just stay here and wait

Because sooner or later, you'll want something from me."

Invisible Woman

"Oh, excuse me, Mrs. I'm trying to get by so I can talk to the pastor. Hey, Pastor, here you go. I made you a cake." Women in the church have a lot of nerves cooking for the pastor and don't even cook for their own husbands and kids. Also, what makes these women think that it's okay to cook for the pastor and think the first lady is going to be cool with that? Many people, especially the women in the church, act as if the first lady doesn't exist. They will talk about the pastor while she's in their presence as if she were not there. The first lady has to listen to congregants having her husband for breakfast, lunch, and dinner, all because he made a decision they didn't agree with. Church folk are very bold. They will even talk about the first lady as if she weren't in the room.

Congregants don't realize that when they hurt the first lady, the pastor hurts too. The first lady often times has to bring it to her husband's attention how much the congregants have hurt her, and once she does, he feels her pain. Yes! The man of God whom they love so much and hold in such high esteem hurts when his wife is hurt by the people whom he has to preach to, love unconditionally, and leave his family to be with their family at the hospital or the cemetery. The pastor has to be almost *surgical* when he handles the hurt of the first lady. He can't just start calling people out over the pulpit. He can't make a public-service announcement about it. So he tries to weave it into his sermons and tries to bring it out while teaching Bible study. If the congregation is not so busy saying amen to everything without hearing what's really being said, they will pick up on what the pastor is trying to tell them. For the first lady to be invisible to the people at the church, she is the most talked about person after the pastor. Many first ladies only find that they can bond with other first ladies, and they are hesitant to do that because they have been so hurt by other church members that church folk turn them off.

No matter how invisible the people try to make her, she continues to make her presence known. She's at most of the church functions. When the pastor has to preach at another church, she's right there on the front row. If other women think they are going to get their claws in the pastor, they must get pass the invisible woman first. It's not as easy getting past someone you pretend not to see.

Because of the fact that the first lady is often overlooked, she had to develop a powerful prayer life. God has anointed her with a spirit of discernment so tough she could call some things out, and God would answer on the spot. Thanks to the congregants ill will toward her, they don't realize they helped create this powerhouse of a prayer warrior. They don't realize that they openly looked over her and she quietly went to God. In her going to God, she gained strength, tough skin, and character. She learned how to roll with the punches. She learned how to see the people's foolishness and yet find something good in them. Always ready to give a hug or an encouraging word, the first lady is a diamond in the rough. She uses being invisible to her advantage. She's a great asset to the pastor and to the church.

Being invisible makes it easy for her to be hidden in God. So when God brings her to the people's eyes, they won't know what hit them. Because she loves the pastor so much and she knows how he feels about the church, she is constantly interceding on their behalf. It costs so much to be the invisible woman. The invisible woman is alone most of the time. The invisible woman gives much and gains little. The invisible woman is misunderstood. The invisible woman always puts herself and her feelings last. Standing on the outside, looking in on the relationship between the first lady and the pastor, one would think she's invisible to him too, the reason being he's always on the go. He's always tending to the needs of others while neglecting the needs of the first lady, so it seems.

She's not invisible to God. He sees her clearly. He sees her heart. He comforts her heart day after day. Because the church treats her like she's invisible, they expect the first lady to take a backseat. God didn't place her in the backseat; he placed her by the side of her husband. She's going to stand by her man no matter what the people say, and she is going to be the first lady when the time comes for the pastor's anniversary. As much as some of them would love to count her out and forget that she even exists, they can't because they would look foolish to every visitor who has come to join in the celebration. Therefore, they give these fake speeches to the pastor and include her as if she cannot see right through them. Yet the first lady smiles and thanks them.

The first ladies who are visible to the church are not the ones with the title "first lady," "elect lady," or "lady." No, she has the title of "pastor" or "co-pastor." If she possesses this title, then she is respected, honored, and looked up to. The congregation tends to hang on to her every word. If she can preach better than her husband, then people tend to want to hear her as opposed to hearing the pastor preach.

If the first lady is the pastor or co-pastor, then more people within the congregation tend to go to her with their problems or suggestions as to how things could be better in the church, thinking that she will make on-the-spot decisions. Her husband is still the head, and she believes in order; therefore, she will not make a decision without consulting with him first. It's funny how a title or a position can change the way the congregation thinks about the most important woman to the pastor.

No One Sees Me

Lord, I walk in this church Sunday after Sunday,
Yet no one sees me.
Lord, I speak,
Yet no one hears my voice.
Lord, I go to hug people,
Yet they don't feel my embrace.
Lord, why don't they hear me, feel me, or see me?
I'm just like them. I just happened
to be married to the pastor.
I have problems like they have.
I have bills like they have.
My kids go through what their kids go through,
Yet they don't see me.
So I'll keep doing what I do and be invisible
Until you decide to show me to them.

Fake Friends and Real Enemies

"Hey, first lady, how are you doing? You were on my mind, and I just wanted you to know that. You're such a graceful lady. I want to be like you when I grow up." Some people say things such as this to the first lady as if she doesn't have an ounce of discernment. They think she doesn't have a clue that everybody who speaks to her is not her friend or even likes her. Mainly, it's some of the women in the church who say these types of things.

First, the first lady was invisible to them; now she's on their mind. Oh! What foolishness and foolish games some women play in the house of God. Some women cozy up to the first lady, wanting friendship, because they think they will gain some kind of clout in the church. Other women try to cozy up to the first lady because they think she's going to reveal something about the pastor or perhaps confide in them so they can use it against her later. They don't even realize that the first lady has guarded her heart and has learned not to speak on such matters to the people whom her husband has to lead.

Those few people who are fortunate enough to be in the first lady's circle are getting vetted on a continuous basis. Some will become very close to her, while others will be branded as "Judas" in her life. The first lady is wise enough to know to keep Judas close to her. As the saying goes, "Keep your friends close but your enemies even closer." The first lady will make sure to love this person in public. She will publicly acknowledge their friendship and place this individual over a committee and sing their praises. All the while, this Judas thinks their getting away with something, and they think first lady is none the wiser.

One thing about having enemies is that they can only hold their peace for so long. They can only act as if they like you for so long. It's just a matter of time before they break their silence and pull the curtain down on their act.

Once this happens, Judas will cause problems and embarrassment for themselves because the whole church has seen how the first lady loved on them, vouched for them, and placed them in position. The church will see how vindictive, malicious, and cruel this person can be.

Many people in the church will start saying, "I don't know why the first lady put him or her in that position anyway. Didn't she know that this person was like that? Didn't she know it was only a matter of time before that person acted up?"

What the people fail to remember is that Jesus picked his disciples and he knew Judas would betray him. God may have told the first lady through prayer to keep Judas around her and appoint them to the position because God has to work something out in that person. Sometimes God has to use our embarrassments to get our attention and to cause a change in us.

The congregation needs to realize that many first ladies didn't want to be in the position they're in. It just so happened that God called their husbands to pastor, and thus, they fell into the role. I haven't seen too many first ladies in my Christian walk, maybe one or two, who welcomed chaos and drama into their lives. But for the most part, many first ladies want peace in the ministry so that their husbands can be in peace and live long healthy lives. They don't want the stress of the church to kill their spouse.

Speaking of dead pastors, first ladies will really know who their enemies are if their husband dies while he's still the pastor of the church. My God, my God! This will be some of the saddest and darkest moments in the church. The congregation will openly mourn the pastor and simultaneously develop a plan to get rid of the first lady. She won't just be contending with the ladies of the church either. She will see how nasty the deacon board and trustee board can be. She will see how the pastor's aide committee is done with her after the funeral. If there is no succession plan in place, she will see the board of directors, elders, bishops, etc., quickly make up some new bylaws, and try to shove them down her throat before the pastor's body is even cold.

However, what the congregation always fails to remember is it's the first lady who has to settle all her husband's affairs. The church can try to do all they want to do, but with a stroke of a pen, a consultation with a lawyer, a bank account full of money, she can throw a wrench into their plans.

After the pastor's death, the first lady is known as public enemy number one in the church. Death can bring out emotions in a person that we never expected, and a grieving first lady is not the enemy you want to deal with. She will remember how the congregation talked about him. She will remember how the congregation would rather spread gossip on her husband than pray for him. She will remember all the times the congregation had treated her badly. Now initially, she will just be concerned about the welfare of her family and her husband's personal belongings. However, when the church lashes out at her and the pastor is no longer around to protect her, she will go into survival mode, and the church will not be prepared for the fury she will unleash on them. But they brought it on themselves.

Being a fake friend is dangerous. It shows that you have no character or integrity. It shows you are willing to stoop very low to gratify yourself. It shows your mask and what's hidden under it. It exposes you to have vengeance released upon you by God when you mess with his children.

WHEN THE WIND BLOWS

It's funny how a little wind blowing on a
hot a sunny day makes us feel good,
But a lot of wind blowing on a cold relationship
bursting at the seams just rips everything to shreds.
Wondering what type of wind it was,
you quickly get on the computer, only to
find your social media pops up.
It clearly describes your wind.
There was the lying wind
There was the cheating wind
There was the gossiping wind
There was the backbiting wind
There was even new wind trying to get into the mix.
When the wind blows,
You must make sure that it is the natural
wind and not the manmade wind.

PART III

Taking the Mask Off

Coming off Life Support

To come off life support means you are ready to breathe on your own. When you allow someone or something to breathe for you and then they decide to walk out or things don't work out, it can take your breath away. When you have no more breath, you become lifeless. It is critical to your survival that you stop letting people determine your quality of life. When someone else determines your quality of life, they have complete control over your mind—the way you think and function. They even have control over your destiny, and God didn't intend that kind of life for you.

When we're on life support, we can be likened to the impotent man in the book of John.

> Now there is at Jerusalem by the sheep market
> a pool, which is called in the Hebrew tongue

Bethesda, having five porches. In these lay a great multitude of impotent folk, of blind, halt, withered, waiting for the moving of the water. For an angel went down at a certain season into the pool, and troubled the water: whosoever then first after the troubling of the water stepped in was made whole of whatsoever disease he had. And a certain man was there, which had an infirmity thirty and eight years. When Jesus saw him lie, and knew that he had been now a long time in that case, he saith unto him, Wilt thou be made whole? The impotent man answered him, Sir, I have no man, when the water is troubled, to put me into the pool: but while I am coming, another steppeth down before me. Jesus saith unto him, Rise, take up thy bed, and walk. (John 5:2-8 KJV)

This man had been impotent for thirty-eight years! He relied on someone else to control his destiny. For thirty-eight years, he sat at the side of the pool, waiting for someone to help him get in. The Bible says he was impotent. It didn't say he couldn't walk, it didn't say he was paralyzed, but it said he was impotent. Dictionary.

com states *impotent* means "not potent, lacking power or ability."

The longer we stay on life support, means the longer we lack the power or ability to think for ourselves, act on our own accord, and take control of our destiny. Even when Jesus himself asked the man if he wanted to be made whole, he was still clinging to the life support of other people, even though they did nothing for him in thirty-eight years. The power that we allow other people to have over us makes us sitting ducks for the enemy to have his way.

Jesus didn't have time to sit and listen to any of this man's excuses; he simply said, "Rise, take up thy bed, and walk." These three steps are so simple but powerful. *Rise*—this is the first step in coming off life support. It's time to build you back up again. It's time to stop looking for someone else to encourage you when you can encourage yourself. It's time to square your shoulders back and say what Job said in Job 13:15: "Though he slay me, yet will I trust in him." It's time to get up from falling after you've been thrown down, called good for nothing, and told you will never be anything without me. *Rise!*

After you've risen, you need to *take up your bed*. Growing up, my mother would always say, "You made your bed. Now lie in it." In other words, to take up your bed means to own your mess and to not blame others for the way you are. We all find it hard to own up to what we've allowed to happen. We tend to leave out the part we've played in the situation that's affecting our lives. Isaiah 6:5 states, "Then said I, Woe is me! for I am undone; because I am a man of unclean lips, and I dwell in the midst of a people of unclean lips: for mine eyes have seen the King, the Lord of hosts" (KJV). Isaiah teaches us that we have to look at the man in the mirror. The reason it was so easy for us to be placed on life support is because we've been hanging with like-minded people. It's right there in the scripture. He said, "I'm unclean and I hang with people that act like me and talk like me." We haven't challenged ourselves to go beyond what we know. I've always been told to have three different types of people in my circle—someone who knows more than me, someone who's on my level, and someone who's beneath me whom I can mentor. By doing this, I can have balance and be challenged to learn more.

The quickest way to take up your bed is to be for real with yourself, take the mask and costumes off, and come clean with God. He already knows what areas in our lives that we've failed at, that we've struggled with, and that we've perfected. He's just waiting on us to say, "Lord, woe is me!" By coming clean, we stop the enemy in his tracks.

He has nothing to hold over us. I've heard someone say, "If I don't talk about it, it cannot become a reality." My response was "It became a reality the minute you failed at it or struggled with it." The question becomes How long are we willing to stay bound, to stay defeated, or to stay on life support when God wants to make us whole?

For many of us, hiding behind our masks and our fear keeps us on life support. If you've been in church for any amount of time, you've quickly learned how to mask up, dress up, and cover up everything. They call it *maturity* when it's really keeping you in captivity. Fear has a way of paralyzing us to the point we don't know how to function in any other way, shape, form, or fashion. As 2Timothy 1:7 says, "For God hath not given us the spirit of fear; but of power, and of love, and of a sound mind." Fear is a spirit, and we have power over it. God gave us *power* (strength, boldness, authority) to accomplish the mission he has for us in life. He's given us *love* (agape, unconditional)—a love that even when we mess up, he's faithful and just to forgive us. He's given us a *sound mind* (discipline mind)—a mind that's stable and fixed on Jesus. When we take firm hold of all this, the spirit of fear cannot rule over us and intimidate us.

Finally, we are told to *walk*. In other words, get moving. It's time to be about our Father's business. It's time to pursue the course of life that God has for us. When you're in the hospital and you've had any type of major surgery or have given birth to a baby, the hospital will not release you until you can walk on your own. When my eldest daughter had her first child, she was a size zero, and the trauma of having a baby took a toll on her body. She could not walk on her own. I asked the doctor for a cane, and I began to walk with her in the hallways at the hospital. The doctor would come into her room and ask, "How are you walking today?" After a while, she didn't need me to help her get the cane and walk the hallways. She was able to do it on her own, and I stood and watched.

Another instance was when I had heart surgery. After the surgery, I was wheeled to my room. The nurse stated, "You have to be able to walk to the bathroom by yourself before the doctor will release you." I went home the same day. I just wanted to make it through the surgery. Once I realized I was still alive, I was ready to go show off the miracle that God had performed. I was back to work in a week.

Many people feel that when God tells them to walk, they have to go at it alone. Christians should know that we're never alone. The Holy Spirit lives inside of us, and he is walking with us. It's just that many Christians neglect the Holy Spirit and treat him like an ordinary man. God will never tell us to do anything and not already have provisions for us to do it. It takes obedience and a willingness of heart to do what God has told us to do. God's not asking us to debate the issue with him. He's not asking us to go get confirmation with what he said. He's not asking us about how many failures we've had in the past. He just wants to know if we are FAT—faithful, available, and teachable.

Get off Your Issues

At what point in life are you going to own your mess? When is it going to stop being everyone else's fault and start being your fault? In getting your life back, you have to take ownership of the good, bad, ugly, and indifferent things you've said and done. In taking ownership, you're showing maturity and growth. We don't want to admit some things because we are ashamed that we've allowed ourselves to do and say some things that we know are not pleasing to God. However, we have to face that man in the mirror and say, "Yes, I've done exactly what people keep saying I did. Yes, I've said exactly what people keep saying I said." In owning up to our faults, we are freeing ourselves and not giving the enemy anything to hold over us.

Isaiah knew this all too well. When King Uzziah died, Isaiah began to do some self-reflection, and he came to the conclusion that he was the one sinning and he hung with a bunch of sinners (Isaiah 6:1-5). He came clean with God. He owned his mess. He didn't care that he was a prophet of God. He didn't let his title keep him in bondage. He didn't let his position in the church keep him in denial. His self-evaluation revealed he was unclean, polluted, and not pleasing to God. Once Isaiah came clean, he was able to answer the call of God, and God could use him.

Wow! What a way to shut the enemy down and gain your freedom. Notice that Isaiah didn't leave out any details when confessing. He didn't play games with God or act as if God didn't already know what he'd been up to.

I've learned to honor the Holy Spirit by confessing my sins to God daily. I just don't say, "Lord, forgive me for all my sins." I name my sins. I call them out before the Lord. Sometimes the Lord even makes me go to the person and apologize even when I've never said what I thought about them. I can remember one time I had to apologize to another sister in the church. I walked up to her and said, "I need for you to forgive me because I have been getting so angry with you, thinking you didn't know how to make a decision for yourself." See, every time I would ask her something, she would always respond. "Let me talk to my husband first." I would smile in her face, but I would be so angry on the inside. I would always say to myself, "You need to get a backbone and learn how to make a decision. Stop relying on someone else to make a decision for you." The Holy Spirit had convicted me so and gave me a revelation on the word submission and a revelation on one of the reason's I'm single. Talk about an eye-opening experience. The word of God had come alive right before my eyes. Thankfully, she forgave me, and our relationship was not hindered by ignorance on my part.

When we choose not to get off our issues, we are saying that we are not willing to grow and that we are okay destroying relationships. Our spiritual growth will be impeded, and it would be a shame to be a child of God all these years and never grow up.

Nobody Wanted to Love Me

I searched for love, high and low.

I even called my friends so we could form a search party;

Some even brought their dogs so that we wouldn't lose the scent.

Love from another was never found.

Therefore, we called off the search party, and everyone went home.

To my surprise, the love I was searching for was at my house.

All I had to do was look deep inside myself and realize love started with me.

Nobody wanted to love me

Because I didn't want to like me;

Nobody wanted to love me

Because I didn't want to love me.

Stop Letting People Turn You Around

It's a dangerous thing to tell everyone your plans, your goals in life, and the promises God made you. When people are not headed in the same direction you're headed or they don't have anything going for themselves, they will give you their opinions and try their best to talk you out of what you're doing. These people will have you dealing with the IRS (insecurities, rejection, sabotage). These people can be your family members, friends, coworkers, or even your sisters and brothers in the ministry. Insecure people lack confidence and always dwell in self-doubt and fear. Everyone has dealt with or is currently dealing with some type of insecurity in their life.

We are afraid to fail. We keep wondering what everyone else is going to say. We wonder what everyone else thinks of us. We look at our bodies and say they don't line up with what society says we should look like, so we starve ourselves and become workout maniacs. Someone said we were not beautiful enough, so we buy hair, nails, designer clothes, and purses to fit society's norms. We go broke, trying to impress people whom we don't like and whom we know don't like us. We rather live in the poor house off credit cards to show people we have status instead of living within our means. Men get muscles because they are tired of women saying they want their man to be like Denzel.

We become afraid and jealous when we learn someone else has the same gift as ours in the church and they seem to work their gift better than we work our gift. That's why you have discord and competition in the church. Or we get jealous of someone else's gift, wishing we had that gift, so we begin to operate out of order. And that's when those Halloween masks and costumes appear.

When you're in the process of getting your life back, you need to be around people who exude confidence, who want to see you do your best in life. Now is not the time to be around people with the "Woe is me" syndrome. Be prepared to be rejected by some of the very people you thought would be happy for you. This may come as a great disappointment for you, but everyone is not happy about you getting your life together. After all, what will they have to talk about once you get your life back? Rejection is painful and can hurt, especially when it comes to close family members and friends.

David knew this all too well. He went to God about this very thing. Psalm 55:12-14 states "For it was not an enemy that reproached me; then I could have borne it: neither was it he that hated me that did magnify himself against me; then I would have hid myself from him: But it was thou, a man mine equal, my guide, and mine acquaintance. We took sweet counsel together, and walked unto the house of God in company" (KJV). David's friend and prayer partner rejected him, talked about him, and didn't believe what God made of him, even though he saw firsthand what God was doing because scripture says they went to church together. God never told us that we would have the support of those around us when he's turning things around in our life.

We would love to have the support of our family and friends, but it's not needed for God to work. That's good news because many of us would never get our lives back if having the support of others were a condition. Rejection can make us want to abort our assignment that God has for us. Rejection has a way of making us stop wanting to be associated with being a Christian, especially when our faith is tested. We'd rather go and blend in with the crowd and get out of character and act like something we're not. Rejection makes us want to put the mask back on and hide.

Sabotage is another thing David dealt with. He was anointed, but Saul was still king. Sometimes you can be anointed by God and have the favor of God on your life, yet someone else is still in the position God anointed you for. Although they're in your position, they are trying to sabotage you because God is still putting your name out there. God is still building you and showing you off, even without being in the position. Saul hated the fact that when David came in from battle, the ladies came out to meet King Saul and David with singing and dancing. They sung, "Saul, you've killed your thousands, and David, you've killed ten thousand." When Saul heard this, he became angry and set out to sabotage David from that day forward (1Samuel 18:6-8). Even in all this, David didn't let this stop him. He still loved Saul and never tried to pay him back for the evil he'd done to him. He was still faithful and wouldn't quit God or the church. He still believed what God had said and didn't allow his circumstances to stop his praise and worship. There are many others in the Bible that dealt with the IRS: Joseph, Moses, Gideon, Samson, just to name a few.

Unfortunately, if you tell the leadership in the church that God has called you and that you are ready to do the work he's called you to do, they begin to sabotage you and tell you you're not ready. Instead of training you, mentoring you, or teaching you, they rather sabotage you and wonder why you're not acting the same. It's in those moments that you have to pray and seek God's face and ask him for directions. This is not the time to gossip and become a hell-raiser in the church because sabotage has come upon you. Now some people will leave the church at this moment, but I suggest you seek the Lord for direction. For if you move out of the will of God, then you are sabotaging yourself.

It Doesn't Matter How You Feel about Me

It doesn't matter what people say
about me or how they feel;
My only goal is to be pleasing to God.
People will act as if they have the authority
to place me in heaven or hell;
They have no idea of the story I have to tell.
I'll testify how God saved me, healed, and delivered me
And not even care how people speak of me.
I've noticed you're mad because I don't follow your ques,
But you were not there when God
touched me in those church pews.
No longer will I follow your lead
nor lean on your might.
I will continue to walk by faith and not by sight.

Stand Firm

When we stand firm on the word of God, it's hard for people to turn us around. *Standing firm* means that we are believing the word, we are trusting God, and we are not wavering. We understand that trials and tribulations are sure to come. No matter what comes our way, we are going to be steadfast and unmovable.

There comes a point in one's life when enough is enough. You get sick and tired of being sick and tired. You're tired of listening to lies the enemy told you. You're tired of caring about what other people think about you. You're tired of being the one trying to please everybody. You've had enough foolishness in your life to last a lifetime. Push has come to shove, and you're ready to do spiritual warfare; fasting and prayer is in full effect. Fasting is no easy thing; you're breaking your flesh down and allowing the Lord to build you back up. When fasting, more than likely we will encounter the spirit of opposition and delay.

War is taking place in heaven on our behalf, and it's just a matter of time before it's manifested in the natural.

Daniel had to deal with this very issue when his prayers were being held up by the enemy, and it took twenty-one days before he received his answer. But his prayers were heard the first day he prayed. As Daniel 10:12-13 says, "Then said he unto me, Fear not, Daniel: for from the first day that thou didst set thine heart to understand, and to chasten thyself before thy God, thy words were heard, and I am come for thy words. But the prince of the kingdom of Persia withstood me one and twenty days: but, lo, Michael, one of the chief princes, came to help me; and I remained there with the kings of Persia" (KJV). When the spirit of opposition and delay arises in your situation, don't give up on God. Don't turn to your friends for advice; continue to stay before the Lord in prayer. Continue to bombard heaven with your prayers. The enemy would love nothing more than for you to give up and throw in the towel. Don't look at opposition in a negative way either. Look at opposition as a way to keep you in communion with God. The more opposition you face, the more you're in the face of God.

Opposition and delay have a way of strengthening your resolve. I know, at first, it doesn't seem like it. But look at the many opportunities it gives God to show up mightily in your life. Look at the many ways you can see for yourself how God will work in your favor. I've learned that when I'm faced with either one of these, God is summonsing me to his face. I've been missing something, and he wants me to pay close attention. He wants more one-on-one time with me without any distractions. He's getting me back to a place in him that I've begun to neglect, and I must nurture it back to life. That place can be prayer, fasting, reading my word, sowing seeds, etc.

Standing firm does not mean you have to act out of sorts. You can still be meek and stand firm; you don't have to be disrespectful to people. Too many people confuse the word *meek* with the word *weak*. When you're meek, you're patient, submissive, and humble. When you're weak, you're fragile, you break, and you lack soundness. When we're being meek, we're saying, I choose to respond and not react. I choose to go to God and see what he has to say about this matter and not react the way the world says I should react. I choose to take a step back and look at the situation from everyone's point of view, instead of reacting like the world and thinking my point of view is the only view. I choose to admit I was wrong in a matter and seek to rectify my wrong doing, instead of reacting like the world and trying to cover up my wrongdoing and act as if nothing ever happened.

When the word of God becomes alive in your spirit, it helps you stand firm and not waiver in your faith, no matter what you're facing on your journey. We must keep in mind that our journey will not be a bed of roses. There will be good days and bad days. It's in those bad days when our faith is tested to the limits that God shows us just what he's placed inside of us. He shows us our strength. He shows us that we're stronger than we thought we were. He shows us that we are more than conquerors through Jesus Christ. He shows us that, even in our weakest moments, he will be strong for us. He shows us that we can take it and we can make it as long as we keep our eyes on him and don't lose hope.

Speak to God for Yourself

When trouble arises, why do we always enlist other people to go to God on our behalf? Why is "Pray for me" the first thing we tell people? Who knows better about the situation—them or us? When trouble arises, we need to speak to God for ourselves. We need to present our own case to our mediator Christ Jesus. We need to make the case why God should intervene on our behalf. Who better to do this than us? People might like us, but they won't fight for us the way we need them to fight for us. I often tell my children, "People like you until you need their help."

The prophet Isaiah came to Hezekiah and told him to set his house in order because he was going to die and he left him after telling him the news. Hezekiah didn't ask Isaiah to pray for him, nor did he call on anyone else in the land. Here's Hezekiah response: "Hezekiah turned his face to the wall, and prayed unto the Lord, and said; remember now, O Lord, I beseech thee, how I have walked before thee in truth and with a perfect heart, and have done that which is good in thy sight. And Hezekiah wept sore" (Isaiah 38:2-3 KJV).

You see how Hezekiah spoke to God on his own behalf. He knew what type of life he lived before the Lord. Hezekiah positioned himself so that he was not interrupted in his prayers. He turned himself to the wall. Before Isaiah could get out the gate, God had him to go back to Hezekiah and say, "I've heard your prayers, I've seen your tears, and I've added fifteen years to your life" (Isaiah 38:5).

One of the most powerful things God gave us was direct access to Jesus. We don't have to tell our problems to the priest and hope they're clean enough to go in the temple before God on our behalf. Since we have direct access to Jesus, why don't we use it at all times?

Hebrews 4:16 states, "Let us therefore come boldly unto the throne of grace that we may obtain mercy, and find grace to help in the time of need" (KJV). Hebrews is letting us know that we don't have to be afraid to come to God for ourselves. We can boldly come to him, we can come to him with confidence, and we can come to him without hesitation. When we speak to God in prayer, we are developing an intimacy with him. How intimate we become depends on each individual.

The more we pray and stay in God's face, the more intimate we become. The less we pray and play hide-and-seek from God, the less intimacy we have. Many relationships among married couples don't last when intimacy is missing. One or both parties go out and cheat and get what they are missing from their partner at home. God is so gracious and kind that when we withdraw our intimacy from him, he doesn't leave us. Jeremiah 3:14 says, "God is married to the backslider" (KJV). Revelation 3:20 goes on to say, "Behold, I stand at the door, and knock: if any man hear my voice, and open the door, I will come in to him, and will sup with him, and he with me."

It's dangerous to ask any and everybody to pray for you. You don't even know if they can get a prayer through to God. You don't know what type of lifestyle they live outside of your presence, and you don't know if they are going to actually pray for you. Let alone, if they pray for you, what type of prayer are they praying?

We should never pass up the opportunity to have a conversation with God. It's just like when you're on your job and it's time for the company to hand out bonuses. Do you want your coworker speaking on your behalf, or do you want to speak with your boss yourself? Your coworker my sell you out if they know they have a chance of getting a piece of your bonus. Besides, who knows how hard you've worked for the company and the lunches you missed to meet a deadline and the early mornings you came in and the late nights you stayed, without complaining? Do you really trust your coworker to highlight that to the boss on your behalf? If so, you trust man more than you trust God.

In talking to a lot of people, many of them have the same testimony: *I don't know how to pray.* I tell them, "Praying is simply communicating with God the same way you and I are communicating." Many people feel that if they don't pray in a loud voice or have some fancy words or pray like the pastor or the intercessory prayer team, then God won't hear them. That's a lie straight from the pit of hell. God hears your silent prayers, and he hears your prayers when you talk to him in a soft voice. We serve a God who's not deaf or blind.

I Have a Voice

When I open my mouth, I'm making a choice
To not let the enemy shut down my voice.
God has empowered me to have a say,
So I will strengthen my faith and begin to pray.
The more I pray, the more I'm learning God's ways.
You just can't say anything to me and think it's okay.
I'm learning the power I possess when I
use the spiritual tools provided to me.
I'm not the weakling you thought
you were going to see.
I'm a child of God, and I know my rights.
I'm no longer depending on you to be my sight.

Allow God to "Unscatter" the Pieces in Your Life

Everyone has some scattered pieces in their life. With some people, you can see all the scattered pieces. With other people, they have their scattered pieces hidden so well that people look at them as if they're perfect. When we don't allow God in every area of our lives, we become dry and brittle in those areas. We experience a spiritual death, and if left unchecked, it can be literal.

> The hand of the Lord was upon me, and carried me out in the spirit of the Lord, and set me down in the midst of the valley which was full of bones, And caused me to pass by them round about: and, behold, there were very many in the open valley; and, lo, they

were very dry. And he said unto me, Son of man, can these bones live? And I answered, O Lord God, thou knowest. Again he said unto me, Prophesy upon these bones, and say unto them, O ye dry bones, hear the word of the Lord. Thus saith the Lord God unto these bones; Behold, I will cause breath to enter into you, and ye shall live: And I will lay sinews upon you, and will bring up flesh upon you, and cover you with skin, and put breath in you, and ye shall live; and ye shall know that I am the Lord. So I prophesied as I was commanded: and as I prophesied, there was a noise, and behold a shaking, and the bones came together, bone to his bone. And when I beheld, lo, the sinews and the flesh came up upon them, and the skin covered them above: but there was no breath in them. Then said he unto me, Prophesy unto the wind, prophesy, son of man, and say to the wind, Thus saith the Lord God; Come from the four winds, O breath, and breathe upon these slain, that they may live. (Ezekiel 37:1-9 KJV)

When we allow God to "unscatter" the pieces in our lives, we have to be obedient to what he tells us to do. He told Ezekiel to prophesy to the bones. That means we have to open up our mouths and speak the word of God to our dry, brittle, decayed, and lifeless areas that persist in our lives. We have to speak life to those scattered pieces. As Proverbs 18:21 says, "Death and life are in the power of the tongue: and they that love it shall eat the fruit thereof" (KJV).

We've been broken and cast down long enough. Every negative thing that could be said about us has been said. Every negative thing that the enemy has tried has failed. It may look like the enemy's winning, but God is in control, and it's only a matter of time before we prevail. Don't speak negativity over your life, and don't allow negative people to speak into your life.

You have to know that everyone is not happy about your deliverance and everyone does not want to see you made whole. You have to keep reminding yourself what God says about you. You have to keep telling yourself, "I'm a child of the king." One word from God is enough to get your life back. One word from God will resuscitate you and restore you to a place in him that you never thought you'd see. God will breathe in you and bring about a spiritual regathering to him. You have to keep telling yourself, "God wanted me that's why he adopted me. God wanted me that's why he sent Jesus to die on the cross for me. God wanted me that's why he didn't divorce me when I walked out on him."

Notice how God allowed Ezekiel to see the dry bones. God will allow people to see you in your state of despair. He will allow people to see how low you are, and some of those people may look upon you and think or even say there's no hope for you. *But God!*

God is going to get the glory out of your life and out of your situation. So don't worry about the people who are watching you go through life's ups and downs. Not only is God showing you his glory, but he's also showing you what he's placed inside of you.

"Unscattering" the pieces of your life means you're ready to let go of the past. You're ready to let go of past hurts, past failures, past disappointments, and past guilt. Sometimes you even have to let go of your past successes so that God can give you new victories, new successes, and new experiences. If we continue to live in the past, how will we ever begin walking toward our destiny? Our mind-sets need to be renewed daily. Our mind-sets have a lot to do with us wallowing in the scattered pieces of our life. We have to become careful not to become so comfortable with the scattered pieces in our lives, that being made whole seems unimaginable. The scattered pieces in our life should make us so uncomfortable that we become determined to breathe again and reach our destiny. As Philippians 3:13 says "Brethren, I count not myself to have apprehended: but this one thing I do, forgetting those things which are behind, and reaching forth unto those things which are before" (KJV).

JIGSAW PUZZLE

Lately, my life seems like a jigsaw puzzle.
I don't know if I'm coming or going.
My mind is here, my mind is there.
My mind is all over the place and everywhere.
I would love for my life to come
together and make sense.
Then I will have to make up my mind
and stop straddling the fence.
I'm tired of all the backbiting, gossiping, and strife.
Lord, I surrender, unscatter all the pieces of my life.

Let Go of the Past

Letting go of the past means you're willing to release control of the memories you thrive on. You're choosing to be free of memories that may have haunted you or reminded you of failures that may have happened. You're choosing not to let past highs be so high that you cannot attain new heights and your lows be so low that you cannot see a better day ahead. Letting go can be one of the scariest things to do, but at the same time, it can be so exhilarating.

It takes faith to let go and walk away from what we're so familiar with, whether it's good, bad, ugly, or indifferent. Other people can look at our situation and say, "Girl, you need to walk away or let that go." It's not until we activate our faith and trust that God got us in every situation that we are ready to let go and run on to see what the end is going to be.

Does letting go hurt? Yes. Does letting go mean you'll never struggle in that area of your life again? No. Does letting go mean your dark days are behind you? No. Depending on who or what you're letting go of, difficulties may follow it. For instance, if you're letting go of an abusive marriage or a bad relationship and children were involved, you may struggle to provide monetarily. Or you may have let go of a great paying job to care for a sick loved one or because you realize a peace of mind is better than any high-figure salary. In the beginning, you may feel as if you've made a terrible mistake. Just know that God sees your pain; he knows your fears, and he has not forgotten about you.

When we decide to hold on to the past, we are deciding to be like a car in reverse. The only time we put our car in reverse is to backup, park, or pull out. In not letting go, we are saying, I want to be parked right here, and I don't want to move forward. I don't want my life to progress, and I'm okay wallowing in my pain and failures. Our failures are not meant to keep us down and hold us back. Our failures are meant for us to learn and grow. Growing hurts. In fact, growing anything naturally or spiritually takes time.

Nonetheless, we can pull out of the past and keep it moving. The beauty of backing up to pull forward is that it's done at a slow pace. No one is asking you to get over it today or tomorrow; however, you need to start the process. You need to learn how to affirm yourself in the areas where someone or something has caused you pain. You need to tell yourself, Today will be better than yesterday. You need to tell yourself; having fear, holding grudges, and planning revenge will not be my character or conduct today. I've let go of the past. Yesterday is gone and never to return. I'm excited about what God has for me in the future, and "This is the day which the Lord hath made; we will rejoice and be glad in it (Psalm 118:24 KJV)."

I'm Trying to Let Go

I want to move on, but my past holds me tight.

I haven't been praying, so I have no power to fight.

Chaos and drama are all wrapped up in a funnel.

Because I won't let go, I can't see the light at the end of the tunnel.

"Just let go," I keep hearing the people say,

But they don't know how bad I've been hurt today.

So I act as if I'm over it for the sake of the show.

If I hold it all in, no one will know.

Why is it so hard to let go? I tend to ponder.

Why not give it to Jesus? He must wonder.

The headaches and heartaches are not worth it—this I know.

Lord, please be patient with me. I'm trying to let go.

OTHER BOOKS

On Your Best Day, You're Well Enough to Die

Don't Love Me to Death: When Teenage Dating
Becomes Deadly

The Lord Is Speaking, but You Might Not Like What
He's Saying

Woman2Woman: A Conversation between Friends

CPSIA information can be obtained
at www.ICGtesting.com
Printed in the USA
BVHW03*1054260718
522720BV00004B/29/P